TRACING
Language Arts 1
Copywork

Easy Peasy

All-in-One
Homeschool

This is just the copywork from Language Arts 1 of Easy Peasy All-in-One Homeschool.

This version has all of the copywork presented as tracing.

This was created for the sake of convenience. Where in the online course it says to copy certain words or sentences, those have been included here. I hope this helps your family.

Where space is available, you could ask your child to rewrite the sentences without the tracing guidelines.

Copyright 2015
Editor Lee Giles
ISBN-13: 978-1515088509
ISBN-10: 1515088502

Lesson 2

His wife shuddered.

Lesson 4

So Jolly Robin thanked

him.

Lesson 6

The struggle was over in a moment.

Lesson 7

On some days there was
no sun at all.

Lesson 8

His wife, however, shook her head.

Lesson 9

He had expected to
have a ride.

Lesson 11

And Jolly Robin did not laugh.

Lesson 13

I'd like to hear you sing!

Lesson 14

And so all the weeping

he might do would be

merely wasted.

Lesson 15

His cousin shook his
head at that.

Lesson 16

The feathered folk in Pleasant Valley were all aflutter.

Lesson 17

But all the others gazed at him in amazement.

Lesson 18

Several times Jasper tried.

Lesson 19

Mr. Crow looked up

quickly.

Lesson 20

Mr. Crow was more than willing.

Lesson 31

That was unfortunate
for the mice.

Lesson 32

It was really a good
thing for Solomon Owl.

Lesson 37

Then Solomon sat up and
listened.

Lesson 40

"What have you been eating?" she inquired.

Lesson 41

"Good!" she exclaimed
with a smile.

Lesson 42

It was different with
Benjamin Bat.

Lesson 44

"What makes you think that?" Benjamin Bat inquired.

Lesson 45

"Oh, I shall be willing to step outside," Solomon told him.

Lesson 47

"You surely ought to be glad to please your own cousin," he told Simon.

Lesson 86

Jolly Robin's worrying wife wouldn't give him a moment's peace.

Lesson 87

Jolly Robin told his wife
how he swooped down
over Reddy
Woodpecker's head.

Lesson 89

One day Reddy was tap, tap, tapping on a tall poplar that grew beside the brook.

Lesson 97

Reddy Woodpecker had
no patience with him.

Lesson 98

It's no wonder Reddy was angry.

Lesson 99

Then Frisky sat up on a limb and glared at him.

Lesson 100

Frisky did not intend to
go hungry when winter
came.

Lesson 106

No, it wasn't that.

Lesson 107

Old Mr. Toad just laughed.

Lesson 108

By and by he turned his
head.

Lesson 110

"Next time I'll get him!"

Lesson 111

ship

shop

shape

shine

shirt

shoe

Lesson 112

"That's good," said she.

Lesson 116

chin
_____

chip
_____

chop
_____

cheap
_____

church
_____

churn
_____

_____

Lesson 119

So Peter hurried over to the nearest tree.

Lesson 121

who

what

why

where

when

which

Lesson 123

By and by, happening to look across the snow-covered Green Meadows, he saw something.

Lesson 124

Peter Rabbit sat in his
secretest place in the
dear Old Briar-patch.

Lesson 126

this _____

that _____

they _____

thing _____

think _____

there _____

_____

_____

Lesson 134

this

thing

where

why

shop

shoe

chop

church

Lesson 136

bikes

stores

cars

tables

friends

times

Lesson 137

washes

misses

brushes

peaches

wishes

taxes

Lesson 138

toys

ways

days

plays

keys

Lesson 141

Who makes an enemy a
friend, to fear and
worry puts an end.

Lesson 142

There the same thing happened.

Lesson 143

A sudden odd surprise
made Farmer Brown's
boy's hair to rise.

Lesson 144

"What is it?" _____

_____

_____

_____

_____

_____

Lesson 145

"That's a splendid idea!"

Lesson 146

shelves

knives

loaves

wolves

leaves

Lesson 150

My favorite place to be
is

Lesson 163

All things bright and
beautiful

Lesson 164

All creatures great and
small

Lesson 165

All things wise and
wonderful

Lesson 166

The Lord God made them all.

Lesson 167

He gave us eyes to see
them

Lesson 168

And lips that we might
tell

Lesson 169

How great is God
Almighty

Lesson 170

Who has made all things

well.

The Easy Peasy All-in-One Homeschool is a free, complete online homeschool curriculum. There are 180 days of ready-to-go assignments for every level and every subject. It's created for your children to work as independently as you want them to. Preschool through high school is available as well as courses ranging from English, math, science and history to art, music, computer, thinking, physical education and health. A daily Bible lesson is offered as well. The mission of Easy Peasy is to enable those to homeschool who otherwise thought they couldn't.

The Genesis Curriculum takes the Bible and turns it into lessons for your homeschool. Daily lessons include Bible reading, memory verse, spelling, handwriting, vocabulary, grammar, Biblical language, science, social studies, writing, and thinking through discussion questions.

The Genesis Curriculum uses a complete book of the Bible for one full year. The curriculum is being made using both Old and New Testament books. Find us online at genesiscurriculum.com to read about the latest developments in this expanding curriculum.

Made in United States
Orlando, FL
07 July 2024

48711028R00037